BOOKS BY CONOR MCPHERSON
AVAILABLE FROM TCG

Dublin Carol

Port Authority

Shining City and *Come On Over*

The Weir and Other Plays

INCLUDES:
The Good Thief
Rum and Vodka
St. Nicholas
This Lime Tree Bower
The Weir

SHINING CITY

INCLUDES

COME ON OVER

SHINING CITY

INCLUDES

COME ON OVER

CONOR MCPHERSON

◄O►

THEATRE COMMUNICATIONS GROUP
NEW YORK
2005

Shining City and *Come On Over* are published by
Theatre Communications Group, Inc., 520 Eighth Avenue, 24th Floor,
New York, NY 10018-4156.

This publication is made possible in part with public funds from the New York State Council on the Arts, a State Agency.

TCG books are exclusively distributed to the book trade by Consortium Book Sales and Distribution, 1045 Westgate Dr., St. Paul, MN 55114.

LIBRARY OF CONGRESS CATALOGING-IN-PUBLICATION DATA
McPherson, Conor.
Shining city : includes Come on over / ConorMcPherson.— 1st ed.
p. cm.
Includes bibliographical references and index.
ISBN-13: 978-1-55936-255-9 (alk. paper)
ISBN-10: 1-55936-255-3 (alk. paper)
1. Widowers—Drama.   2.   Spiritualism—Drama.
3. Dublin (Ireland)—Drama. 4. Psychotherapist and patient—Drama.
I. McPherson, Conor. Come on over.   II. Title.
PR6063.C73S55   2005
822'.913—dc22   2005023672

Cover photo by Conor McPherson
Author photo by Fionnuala Ní Chiosáin
Cover, book design and composition by Lisa Govan

First Edition, December 2005
Second Printing, January 2007

For my wife
Fionnuala

CONTENTS

—◄o►—

SHINING CITY

PRODUCTION HISTORY

Shining City was first performed at the Royal Court Theatre in London on June 4, 2004, and then at the Gate Theatre in Dublin on September 23, 2004. The director was Conor McPherson, the designer was Rae Smith, the lighting designer was Mark Henderson and the sound designer was Ian Dickenson. The cast was:

IAN	Michael McElhatton
JOHN	Stanley Townsend
LAURENCE	Tom Jordan Murphy
NEASA	Kathy Kiera Clarke

IAN, forties
JOHN, fifties
NEASA, thirties
LAURENCE, twenties

Setting

The play is set in Ian's office in Dublin, around Phibsboro maybe, or Berkeley Road, an old part of the city which, while it retains a sense of history, is not a salubrious area. It has a Victorian feel, lots of redbrick terraced houses dominated by the Mater Hospital, Mountjoy Prison, and the church spires of Phibsboro Church and the church at Berkeley Road. It doesn't feel like a suburb, if anything it feels like a less commercial part of the city center, which is only a short walk away.

Ian's office is perhaps in an older, larger building than most in the area, up on the third floor. From his elevated position, at the back of the building, one or two church spires loom outside.

There is a big sash window at the back. There are some shelves with books on them. A stereo and some CDs. There are more books on the floor, as though they have been unpacked but have yet to be put away. Ian has a desk, stage left-ish, with a chair behind it. There is also a chair in front of the desk which Ian uses for sitting with clients. Clients sit on a little two-seater sofa near the middle of the room, a little more stage right. There's a coffee table near the sofa with a box of tissues and a jug of water.

At the back, stage right, is a door to a little bathroom. Stage right is a cabinet of some kind, a filing cabinet maybe, or a bookcase.

The door is stage right, and when it is open we can see out to the banister and the top of the stairs. Beside the door is a handset for an intercom to the main door to the street on the ground floor.

The play has five scenes and about two months elapse between each scene.

The time is the present.

A NOTE ON SCENE CHANGES

I would prefer if stage management did not appear on stage during scene changes. In the original production the actor playing Ian made any necessary arrangements in the room, carrying furniture and objects on and off by himself.

We made a virtue of the scene changes using them to indicate the passage of time. As Ian changed his costume or brought some new objects into the room we indicated days and nights going by. From dawn rising to noon, to early afternoon, to late afternoon, to dusk and nighttime, over and over while music played. When the work was complete the music faded and the next scene began. It enabled us to get a sense of Ian's life continuing . . .

There was no interval.

The music we played was:

Before Scene One: "Polly" by Gene Clark
Between Scenes One and Two: "Through the Morning, Through the Night" by Gene Clark
Between Scenes Two and Three: "Fair & Tender Ladies" by Gene Clark

Between Scenes Three and Four: "Razor Love" by Neil Young
Between Scenes Four and Five: "Polly" by Gene Clark
(which is the CD Ian puts on in the play)

All Gene Clark tracks are available on *Flying High* (Universal/Polygram, 1999). The Neil Young track is from the album *Silver & Gold* (Warner Brothers, 2000).

—CMP

SCENE ONE

As the lights come up there is no one onstage. It is daytime. We hear distant church bells. Music is playing softly on the stereo. We hear the toilet flush, and Ian, a man in his forties, comes out of the bathroom. He takes a tissue from the box and goes to the window, blowing his nose. He is a man who has struggled with many personal fears in his life and has had some victories, some defeats. The resulting struggle has made him very sharp. He is essentially a gentle man, but sometimes his desire to get to the lifeboats, to feel safe, drives him in ways that even he himself doesn't fully understand. A loud, ugly buzzer goes off. Ian turns off the stereo and goes to the intercom, picking up the handset.

IAN: Hello? *(Pushing a button on the intercom)* Okay, come in.

(Pause.)

Are you in? Okay. *(Pushing the button)* Push the door. Are you in?

(Pause.)

Hello? No? Okay, okay, hold on.

(He hangs up the handset and goes out, leaving the door open. He goes down the stairs.)

(Off) Now.

JOHN *(Off)*: Sorry.

IAN *(Off)*: No, I'm sorry. Come on up. Yeah. It was fixed. I don't know if all this rain . . . We're all the way up, I'm afraid.

JOHN *(Off)*: Straight on?

IAN *(Off)*: Eh, the next one. Yeah. And that's it there. The door is open.

(John comes in. He is in his fifties and dressed quite respectably. He has an air of confusion when we first see him, not just because of his recent experiences but also because he has yet to accept that the world is not as orderly and predictable as he thought. He has always found problems to arise from what he regards as other people's ignorance. He almost regards himself as a benchmark for normality. He carries an anorak. He seems very tired. Ian follows him in and indicates for him to have a seat on the sofa.)

Now, right.

JOHN *(Sits)*: Thanks.

IAN *(Sits)*: I'm sorry about that.

JOHN: No, sure I wasn't sure I had the right . . . I was in a bit of a flap, God, the parking around here is horrendous, isn't it?

IAN: I know.

JOHN: I left myself a bit of time but I was almost like a curbcrawler out there looking for a spot.

IAN: I know. I tell you I'm only here, I've only been here two weeks, and I'm not sure . . . between ourselves . . . that I'm going to ... *(He nods)* because there's ... many disadvantages ...

JOHN: Ah, no, I parked up in the hospital in the end, which is what I should have done in the first place. I'll know the next time. It's my own fault.

IAN: No, I know, I should have probably ... But like I say, I'm still sort of only getting myself sorted out here but I should have ...

JOHN: Ah sure no, it's grand, sure I'm here now.

IAN: Yes! Well good.

JOHN: Yeah, well that's the main thing ... Can I eh ... *(Indicates water)*

IAN *(Indicates affirmatively)*: Please.

(John pours himself some water and drinks a few mouthfuls. Ian reaches around behind him and takes a letter from his desk.)

So ... *(Glancing at letter)* John ... *(Pause)* How are you?

JOHN: Not too bad. A bit ... Eh ... heh ... eh ... I've never ... ehm ... been to see ... someone before ...

IAN: All right. Well that's okay.

JOHN: Em ... *(He doesn't seem to know where to begin)*

IAN: I got a, I have a letter ...

JOHN: Right.

IAN: From Dr. Casey ...

JOHN: That's right. Yeah, he was ... there was some guy he wanted me to see and ... we couldn't get an appointment, for four months or something!

IAN: Okay.

JOHN: Yeah, so ...

IAN: And you haven't been sleeping so well. Is that right?

JOHN: Well, yeah ...

(Pause.)

IAN: Which can be very debilitating, I know.

JOHN: Yeah . . . and ehm . . . *(He holds his hand up to the bridge of his nose as though he is about to sneeze and there is silence. He is silently crying)* Can I . . . ? *(He indicates tissues)*

IAN: Of course. Please.

JOHN *(Composes himself)*: Sorry.

IAN *(Reassuringly)*: That's fine. That's fine.

JOHN: You have the tissues ready and everything.

(They smile.)

I'm em. I'm recently bereaved. I don't know if Dr. Casey . . .

IAN *(Affirmative)*: Mm-hm.

JOHN: My wife passed away a few months ago. And em . . .

(Pause.)

She . . . she, she died in em, horrible circumstances, really, you know?

IAN: Okay.

JOHN: She was in a taxi. And a . . . stolen car crashed into them. And she was . . . trapped, in, the car. It was a, a horrific crash, and she . . . didn't, she couldn't survive. And I was on my . . . I was too late getting to the hospital. And the eh . . . reality of . . . the reality of it. It's been absolutely . . . It really, now . . . It's . . . *(He nods)* You know . . .

(Pause.)

IAN: I can em . . . I can only imagine what . . .

JOHN: We have no children. And eh . . . *(Pause)* And I've eh . . . been on my own an awful lot, you know? Like, I've really been on my own an awful lot of the time, really, you know?

IAN: Okay.

JOHN: And I don't . . . I mean I don't even know where she was that night, you know? Or where she was coming from. Do

you know what I mean, you know? Like we weren't even . . .
communicating. At the time, do you understand me?

IAN: Okay.

JOHN: And no one else was injured. And I've no . . . idea . . . wh . . .
(Long pause) But, em, I've . . . em . . . I've seen her. *(Short pause)* I've em . . .

IAN: Sorry. You've seen her?

JOHN: I've seen her in the house. She's been in the house.

IAN: You've . . .

JOHN: Yeah.

IAN: This is . . .

JOHN: Yeah.

IAN: Since . . .

JOHN: Yeah, since . . .

IAN: Since she . . .

JOHN: Yeah since she . . .

IAN: Sorry, go on . . .

JOHN: Yeah, no, she em . . . about eh, about two months ago. I . . .
met up with my brother, I have a brother, Jim, and we met
one evening, for a pint in Clontarf Castle. We're just, are we
just going into this? You just . . .

IAN: Well, no, just whatever you want, you just tell me . . . in your
own, we don't have to, you can . . . You're telling me so, I'd
like to . . .

JOHN: No I just, I wasn't sure if, but, you know, we . . . my brother,
you know, we don't, we haven't . . . eh . . . I don't see him. You
know, to a certain degree, we've been out of contact. He only
lives in Clontarf. But for . . . you know . . . he . . . but since
the . . . funeral . . . He, you know, we've had contact again.
And it's fine, you know. But for a long time . . . he's been very
supportive, but you know we don't get on, basically, you
know? And I don't . . . there's no need for me . . . to infringe
on his privacy and his family. And you know, so we've drifted
again. But em, the . . . the last time that I saw him, this night
that I'm talking about a couple of months ago. I mean, I could

feel . . . that . . . it was a sympathy vote, like . . . we'd . . . very little to . . . to say to each other. And I mean, he's very quiet anyway, you know? And I . . . didn't feel . . . right, myself that evening, anyway and . . . And I mean, there was no . . . problem, as such. But I . . . just wanted to leave, you know? And I kind of just got a bit annoyed and I kind of . . . fucking . . . just went home, you know?

(He checks with Ian, to see if this is all all right to continue with. Ian nods gently.)

And eh . . .

And I didn't really . . . when I got home, there was nothing untoward when I got in the door. Only that I remember now, because I heard it again, there was the sound, the tune of an ice-cream van. The music, you know? But there couldn't have been because they don't go round at night. But, I heard it when I got in the door. And I . . . didn't think about it or . . . But eh . . . I was, I was just going into the living room and I put the lights on, and . . . when I turned around I could see that she was standing there behind the door looking at me.

(Pause.)

IAN: Your wife?

JOHN: Yeah. She . . . I could only see half of her, behind the door, looking out at me. Eh . . . but I could see that . . . her hair was soaking wet, and all plastered to her face. And I, I fucking jumped, you know? And I fucking just stood there, I froze, it was terrifying. And I mean she was as real as . . . you know if you've ever seen a dead body? How strange it is, but . . . it's . . . real! That feeling . . .

IAN: And what happened then?

JOHN: I just, I don't know how long we were standing there looking at each other. I mean it might have been only a few seconds. But it was like if you're a kid and you get a fright, it's only for a second, you know, if you have a bad dream or you think you see something, but then, you wake up or there's nothing there or whatever, but this just didn't stop, I mean she was just there, and it was real. The feeling is like . . . I mean, I mean it's unbelievable, you know? It's . . . it's . . . I can't describe it.

IAN: And did she . . . did you . . .

JOHN: Well finally, I don't know how, but I just got my legs going and I just had no choice and I just went straight out the door, straight by her, I mean the door was open, she was behind it, and I just went straight out and right out of the house. (*Pause*) And then, of course, I was just standing in the garden with no coat on, with really no fucking idea what I was doing, you know? So I just got in the car. (*Pause*) And I kind of just sat there. Where I live is just a quiet cul-de-sac. There wasn't anyone around even that I could . . . even the neighbors, I've never, you know, those people . . . I just sat there, looking at the house, just so . . . frightened, you know? And . . . there was just nothing I could do. So I just drove away. (*Short pause*) Just down to this B and B. Bec . . . because I . . . I just didn't want to be on my own like. (*Short pause*) The woman there, I'd say she knew there was something weird going on all right. I had no luggage and it was so late. She probably thought I'd had a row, you know?

IAN: You didn't go to your brother?

JOHN: No. (*Pause*) He's . . . we'd, we'd had a . . . I mean I'd walked out on him, earlier, you know? . . . No.

IAN: Did you tell anyone? Is there anyone that you . . . who you . . .

JOHN: No, I . . . I . . . I just . . . I just went back the next day, you know? I . . . I just, I suppose, I made myself, I refused to . . . the next morning it was like, "What the fuck am I doing?" You know? I mean you just don't know what to do. I rang them in work and said I wouldn't be in, because I sort of

knew if I didn't go back . . . I mean when it gets bright you
just . . . For some reason I was, I was just able to go back.

IAN: But you didn't talk to anybody about what had happened?

JOHN: No. I suppose I should have but . . .

(Silence.)

IAN: And did you see . . . her again? Or . . .

JOHN: Yeah, no, well the next time I didn't . . . see anything,
I was in the bath, and . . .

IAN: When, how long was this, after . . .

JOHN: Two . . . days later, you know, not long . . .

IAN: Okay.

JOHN: I figured, you know, I, I rationalized it, that maybe . . . I
hadn't . . . seen her or . . . Like there was nothing there! And
I thought maybe it . . . that . . . just the fucking grief I suppose . . . you know . . .

IAN: Of course.

JOHN: You might say it's mad, but what choice did I have?

IAN: No.

JOHN: I mean, I have to get on with my life!

IAN: I know.

JOHN: So yeah, there I was, having a bath. It was fairly late. And
I was just trying to relax. I had the radio on. I was listening
to Vincent Browne. And the door was closed. I had . . . I had
locked it. It's stupid 'cause there was . . . I was there on my
own, but, I don't know. It's just a habit or it made me feel a
bit better, you know, more safe. And I was lying there and
I thought I, I thought I heard something, you know? Like . . .
someone in the house. Just not even a noise, just a feeling.
You can just feel, you know, don't you? When someone is
there. But I, I just turned off the radio, just to see if . . . and
then I heard her, she was knocking on the door and going . . .
(He bangs his fist urgently on the wooden arm of the sofa)
"John! John!"

IAN: Oh my God.

JOHN: Yeah! So I, I leapt up out of the bath, and I slipped, and I took an awful . . . I went right over and really bruised my hip and my shoulder, and by the time I had sorted myself out, I got a grip and I . . . eventually, opened the door, but of course, and I know you're going to think I was dreaming or whatever, there was nothing there. But it was absolutely terrifying. And at the same time I was completely frantic, do you understand me?

IAN: Well, of course you were. What, what did you . . .

JOHN: Back down to the B and B! What could I do?! *(Pause)* I'm still there!

IAN: You're still . . .

JOHN: I'm living there! What can I do?

IAN: I know.

JOHN: I mean I have to sell the house! That's where I'm at, you know? I'm not working. I'm completely on my own. I mean the woman in the B and B doesn't know what to make of me. I mean she's very nice and everything, but what can I say to her? I told her I'm getting work done. And her husband is a builder, and he was asking me all these questions one morning. And I know nothing about it, you know? I think they think I'm a nutcase!

(Silence.)

IAN: Okay. *(Pause)* Well . . .

JOHN: Do you believe me?

IAN *(Taking up a writing pad)*: Well, let's, let me get some details, is that all right?

(John nods.)

How old are you, John?

JOHN: Fifty-four.

IAN: And what do you do?

JOHN: I'm a . . . I'm a rep for a catering suppliers . . . on an independent basis . . .

IAN: And have you . . .

JOHN *(Interrupting Ian)*: Wait. Do you believe me?

IAN: . . . had any . . . sorry?

JOHN: Do you believe what I'm saying to you? That this is happening to me?

(Pause.)

IAN: I believe you . . . that . . . I believe something is . . . I believe you, in that I don't think you're making it up.

JOHN: I'm not making it up.

IAN: Yes but . . . I believe you're telling me you saw something, but if you're asking me if I believe in ghosts, I . . .

JOHN: Yeah but can you help me with this? Because . . . *(His voice suddenly cracks)* I really don't know what the fuck I'm going to do here . . . *(He puts his hand to his mouth)*

(Pause.)

IAN: I know. I know. Don't worry. You're not on your own now, okay? We'll sort it out.

(Pause.)

Don't worry.

(Short pause.)

Don't worry.

(Lights down.)

SCENE TWO

It is night. Ian and Neasa are in the office. Perhaps she sits on the clients' couch. Maybe at the beginning it looks like a therapy session. She is in her thirties and is more working class than Ian. She is rooted in a harder, less forgiving reality. She has always had a stubbornness which has kept her focused, but has also sometimes blinded her so that, while she is a strong person, often it is others who have used her strength.

NEASA: Are you fucking joking me, Ian?

IAN: No, I'm . . .

NEASA: No, no no no no no no . . .

IAN: Look, I know, but . . .

NEASA: No no no— *(As though it's so obvious)* —you come home now.

IAN: Neasa, I'm . . . I'm just not going to do that. *(He goes to the desk and takes a cigarette from a pack)*

NEASA: No. Because people have fights, Ian, and everybody hates
it—but you know you have to do it sometimes, you know?
That's . . . Please don't smoke, Ian, 'cause it'll make me want
to smoke.

IAN: Okay! What's that smell?

NEASA: It's new . . . stuff for the . . . thing . . . on my leg.

IAN *(Beat)*: And this is not because we had a fight! What do you
think I am?! I know that people have fights—this is not
because . . . It's not because I'm "hurt" or something—it's,
it's because . . .

NEASA: Oh, it's not because you're hurt, no? It's not because you're
sulking and you've been letting me stew in my own juice for
four days, no?

IAN: No I haven't actually—I've been trying to just fucking
think about what I need to figure out what I need to do, you
know?

NEASA: But you couldn't phone me, to tell me that, no? You just
let . . . me just . . .

IAN *(Shouts)*: Anytime I thought about phoning you I knew that
it would just turn into this! We said, both of us said that we
should give it a bit of time to . . . but oh no . . .

NEASA *(Shouts)*: I didn't know you were going to leave me on my
own for a whole week, and I didn't even know where you
were!

IAN: It's not a week, it's a couple of days, Jesus!

NEASA: It's not just a couple of days when you're on your own
with a baby—it's completely fucking exhausting not knowing where you are—and I can't fucking do it!

What am I supposed to say to your brother? He hasn't
even asked me where you are! No one knows what to say.
—Of course she's delighted—she hates me—they think
I've ruined your life. She's delighted with herself that I'm
sitting up there on my own—she's so fucking smug now!

IAN *(Annoyed, embarrassed, dismissive)*: It doesn't matter what
they think.

NEASA: That's easy for you to say! I have nowhere to fucking go! It's their house! What right do I have to stay there if you're not there?

IAN: It's none of their business!

NEASA: What do you mean it's none of their business? You don't know what it's like! I'm sitting up there on my own in the boxroom with the baby, they don't even come near me. And I can't go downstairs! You should have seen the face on her when I asked her to mind Aisling tonight! *(Shouts)* You don't know what it's like!

IAN: Look! This is all . . . getting sorted out! I nearly have a thousand euros in the bank—if you just let me get on with my work, if you just let me do it my way, you'll have your own place, there'll be no more of this and we can get on with it, but if you're going to . . . *(Unsaid: "harass me")* I can't . . . *(Unsaid: "work")*

NEASA: What do you mean, my own place?

IAN: Can you not see that this is happening?! I don't . . . want . . . I can't . . . I can't . . . I can't . . . I don't . . . I don't want this relationship anymore!

NEASA: What the fuck are you talking about? What the *fuck* are you talking about?

IAN: God! Can you not hear me?! Can you not listen to what I'm saying?

NEASA: I don't know if I can! Because have you completely lost touch with reality? Have you completely fucking lost touch with fucking reality?

IAN: This is reality!!

NEASA: What are you talking about? What about the baby?!

IAN: But this is not about the baby!

NEASA: What are you talk— How can it not be about the baby?!

IAN *(Shouts)*: Because it's not about that! Because it's about that *I* can't continue with *you*! With you and me!

NEASA: But what do you mean? What have I done? What have I done?

IAN: It's not what you've *done* or what I've *done*. It's . . . It's . . .

NEASA: What . . . What, Ian . . .

IAN: IT'S BECAUSE I CAN'T DO IT!

(Pause.)

NEASA: I knew this. I knew this was going to happen. I knew it. I knew it.

IAN: Look, if you'd just listen to me for once, and hear something that goes in, we're going to get you out of my brother's house. It's all going to be sorted out and I'm earning some money now and everything.

NEASA: Yeah, now that it's all . . . Now you're on your feet. My father fucking said this to me, you know? He fucking said it to me. A priest . . . ?

IAN: I'm not a . . . !!

NEASA: An ex-priest? Forget it—he said anyone who goes next or near the priests is a fucking headache to begin with. But I wouldn't listen to him!

IAN: Oh yeah, and your dad is a real one to know.

NEASA: Yeah, he's a drunk. But he's a human being, you know? He has feelings—he knows things, you know?

IAN: Yeah, well, is your father going to find you somewhere to live?

NEASA: Oh yeah, like you really found us somewhere to live, Ian. Squashed into your brother's house with that fucking bitch always fucking looking at me like I'm going to rob something, like she has anything . . .

IAN: Wait, now, don't fucking . . . What did you think was going to fucking happen?! I said it to you, I have to start all over again and it's gonna be tough! *(Sarcastic)* Of course you didn't know that—you didn't know any of that!

NEASA: Yeah but I didn't think that at the end of it all you were . . . *(Despair, bewilderment)* Are you breaking it off with me?! *(Pause)* I was just thinking about it. Do you remember the week you left the order—about . . . a day later, you were so worried about money, I'd say like a *day* later— I *immediately* started working all the extra shifts I could get. I kept having to lick up to that sleazy bollocks Darren, just to keep working in that fucking *kip* of a pub . . .

IAN: Look, I know, I know that.

NEASA: Just so you wouldn't have to worry about anything! No one could understand how I put up with the things that he said to me in front of people. But I did it so you could have the money for your course!

IAN: I know. I know. And . . . look . . . I'm . . . going to do everything that I can. And, I promise, I'm going to look after you, you know?

NEASA *(Shouts)*: But I don't want for you to "look after" me! I never wanted for anyone to have to look after me! I even said—when I got pregnant—I even said then we should leave it and we should wait until we have some more money. I said, "This is too soon." YOU SAID, "NO," YOU SAID, "NO, NOT TO DO THAT!" Because you thought it was "wrong"! Now look! *(Short pause)* What am I going to do? How can I go back there on my own again tonight? What am I going to say to your brother?

IAN: Don't say anything to him. I'll talk to him.

(She stands there. She is ruined.)

NEASA: What am I going to do?

IAN: Can you not go back around to your granny, even for a few . . . ?

NEASA: My dad is back there!

(Ian throws his eyes to heaven, as if this is an endless saga.)

IAN *(Beat)*: Look, I know. I know that this . . . seems . . . like . . . but . . . this is the worst point, you know? And I've . . . I know

I've made some huge mistakes, and I'm the first person who'll say that, you know? But I've got to put it right, and I'm going to put it right. But we can't continue like this and . . .

NEASA: Ian, I don't think I can do this on my own. I didn't think that this was going to happen.

IAN: I know but . . . you're not on your own. I'm with you in this, you know?

NEASA: But what are you saying to me?

IAN *(Calmly, reasonably, almost sweetly)*: Look. Aisling is our daughter. And I'm her father and you're her mother. And I fully . . . you know? I want to be her father and . . . be, you know . . . but you and I . . . are breaking up. And that's all, you know? That's all that's happening here. That's all it is.

NEASA: How can you say that? How can you say that that's all it is? Can you see what this is doing to me?

IAN: I know. But we can't . . . I . . . can't . . .

NEASA: Do you not love me anymore?

IAN: I . . . I'll always . . . I mean, you have been . . . you were the only . . . when . . . when it was all so hard for me . . . And I had to make that big decision—and it was a *huge* thing for me— *(As though he has accomplished something completely unthinkable)* —to turn my back on the Church?!—that was a *huge* thing for me. You were there for me, and I couldn't have come through it without you. I just couldn't have done it, I just couldn't have, you know? But . . . the fucking huge mistake I made was thinking that that was the end of the journey for me—and it wasn't.

(Pause.)

NEASA: Have you met somebody else?

IAN: No, no I haven't. I promise you. It's not that . . . *(Pause)* I can't stay with you, with us, I can't do it. But I'm going to make sure that you want for nothing.

NEASA: But I just don't understand any of this. I just can't believe that it's happening even, you know?

(She takes a bottle of wine from her bag.)

I bought this this afternoon because I thought we were going to make up, and then you were going to come home with me.

(She is shaking with fear and dread.)

IAN: I'm sorry. I'm sorry. I'm sorry.

(Silence.)

NEASA: Is this . . . Is this because of me and Mark Whelan?
IAN: What?

(Pause.)

NEASA: Is it because . . .
IAN: Because what? *(Pause)* Because what? *(Pause)* What do you, what are you . . . ?
NEASA: Look, it doesn't matter, okay? Forget I asked.
IAN: No, wait, hold on. What do you mean is this because of you and Mark Whelan? What about you and Mark Whelan?
NEASA: Please, Ian, just . . . Please . . .
IAN: What do you mean it doesn't matter? What doesn't matter?
NEASA: Nothing, just . . . because I wanted just to ask you . . . if that was why.
IAN: But why are you asking me that? Did you . . .
NEASA: Ian, please, I'm asking you not to ask me about this now, please!
IAN: Not to ask you about what though?

(Pause.)

23

Not to ask you about what?

(Pause.)

I'm not . . . *(Unsaid: "surprised")* Because, do you remember,
I asked you about him before.

NEASA: And I told you.

IAN: You said there was nothing going on!

NEASA: There wasn't . . . then, when . . .

IAN: So what? Have you something you want to tell me?

NEASA: It doesn't make any difference, Ian, please, believe me.
I just wanted to know if it was because . . .

IAN: Yeah, but, like I mean, what?

NEASA: Please, Ian. Please, I'm asking you, okay?

IAN: Yeah, but . . . I mean . . . wait a minute . . . What about you
and Mark Whelan, you know? *(Pause)* Have you had sex
with him?

*(Pause. She doesn't know what to say—all she knows is that it
feels like her world is ending.)*

That's a "yes" then, I suppose then, yeah?

(Pause.)

NEASA: Can you not see what this is doing to me, Ian? Can you
not see what this is doing to me? You're doing it anyway, Ian,
you're leaving me anyway. Please don't leave me, please
don't do it.

*(Ian knows that he shouldn't continue with this, but he can't help
it. He feels angry, frightened, powerless, but also adrenalized.)*

IAN: Yeah, but you know what? This is fucking . . . You're throw-
ing the baby in my face . . . and you're screwing around!

NEASA: I'm not!

IAN: But it's like I'm the one who, you know, that I . . .

NEASA: It was before the baby, Ian, I wasn't screwing around!

IAN: When before the baby? Just before?

NEASA: No, she's our baby Ian, no!

IAN: Is she? I mean, wh . . . because I don't *know* . . . anything, here.

(Pause.)

Because I was shocked when you got pregnant, we both were. I thought we both were.

NEASA: No, no no no, she's your baby, she's your baby, she's yours and mine—this is crazy! Just, you have to believe me. Don't even . . .

IAN: Look, wait, hold on, hold on. This is . . . What are we talking about here?

(Pause.)

NEASA: Nothing. Really. Nothing. There was just . . . no one to talk to and—

IAN *(Interrupting)*: When?

NEASA: Just in, all around that time. When you came out and you were freaked-out all the time, and you were starting your course. And I was working all the time. I just couldn't . . . keep going back up to your brother's house on my break, with her always there, Ian, it was horrible.

IAN: You know they've been so good to us really when you think about it, you know that?

NEASA: I know but, I was just always on my own!

IAN: But you weren't! When?

NEASA: I just . . . I didn't have anyone even that I could just have a normal talk to.

(Pause.)

I just feel like it's all my fault now, you know? And I was . . . I was worried all the time about everything, even then, you know? Mark just, would always ask me if I was all right, and how I was getting on . . .

IAN: Oh, I never asked you how you were? I'm just a fucking animal, yeah?

NEASA: I just believed him, when he asked.

(Pause.)

IAN *(Dismissive)*: Yeah, well.

NEASA: I didn't know what was going on. It was just like things were supposed to get better and they just kept getting worse and worse. I couldn't go back up there on my break. She always was saying something about the smell of smoke off me. I was working in a pub! You know? What did she want me to do? And . . . I started going around to Mark's flat—I told you, I told you I was doing that.

IAN: Yeah but . . .

NEASA: Yeah, well, I didn't . . . I didn't know that . . . anything . . . was . . . going to happen. I didn't think that there was even anything like that with him . . . But one day he was . . . he didn't say anything to me . . . We just got in the door and I just knew that . . . what he was . . . I didn't know what to do. I just, I only kind of realized when we got in the door that . . . he was . . . It was just really, I didn't . . . it was just really quick and it was, I didn't even want to do it. We both felt terrible after it. I'm sorry, Ian. I'm sorry. It was only once. It was only one time. It wasn't anything, really. And I've never gone there after.

I'm sorry, Ian.

I don't love him, Ian. I never loved him. I only ever wanted to be with you. Really. Really.

And I don't know what happened.

Say something. Say something to me, will you?

(Long pause.)

IAN: I'm sorry.

(Silence.
Neasa starts to get her stuff together. She leaves the bottle
of wine.)

NEASA: I better go. 'Cause I'm gonna miss the last bus.
IAN: Look. I'll . . . I'll call you tomorrow, and . . .
NEASA *(Almost silently)*: Yeah.

(She goes to the door.)

IAN: Neasa.

(She pauses.)

Look, I'm . . .

(Pause.)

NEASA: It's not your fault.

(She leaves. He stands there.
Lights down.)

SCENE THREE

Lights up on the office. It is the afternoon. The door is open and there is no one in the office. There is a bit more furniture around the place, maybe a plant or two. John comes in and stands there. He looks a bit better than he did in Scene One, and there is something more focused about him, he means business. Ian follows him in.

IAN *(Slightly exasperated)*: Well, I don't know . . .

JOHN: I'm sorry, God, I can never . . .

IAN: No! You know I've asked them every single week, and they say they have a caretaker who keeps missing me. I think it's a total spoof.

JOHN: Don't give them the rent.

IAN: You think?

JOHN: They'll be round in a flash. That's the language they speak, you know. Money talks in this town. It rules really, you know?

IAN: God, tell me about it! Keeps me fit anyway, going up and down the stairs.

JOHN: Yeah! Well . . .

(John really has his bearings in the office now. He throws his jacket over a chair and sits, unbidden, on the sofa, pouring himself a glass of water. Ian sits.)

IAN: So . . . how are you?

JOHN: Yeah, well I'm . . . this helps, you know . . .

IAN: Good, good . . .

JOHN: I, you know, I focus around it. It's been a good week em . . . They're, you know still very good about everything at work, there's no pressure to go in . . . em . . . the time is . . . good . . . it's . . .

(Pause.)

IAN: Are you sleeping or . . .

JOHN: Well, the same really. You know, I do . . . get a few hours. But, it's like there's something in me's determined to keep me up all night, you know? I never go off till around five, six, even. Then, of course, nine o'clock, the woman knocks on the door so I won't "miss breakfast." God forbid! You know?

(They smile.)

So . . . of course I'm in bits but, I get up, go down. I'm always the last. She usually has a few staying there, but, they're on business or whatever, they're . . . they're gone out, you know? So, I sit there, watching the traffic outside, and . . . I have an egg, cup of coffee . . . Get myself going then . . . you know . . .

IAN: You're still getting your walk in . . .

JOHN: Rain or shine. I get out, go down the coast. Down as far as the Bull Wall. The B and B is more the Fairview end so, you know, it's a good walk . . . Get the paper, throw any stuff into the laundry there. There's a little café next door, there near the Dollymount House. So, you know . . . that's . . . been the little routine, but I've em . . . I've bitten the bullet and done what you suggested. Couple of mornings I got in the car, dropped into the house, you know?

IAN: Okay. So, how is that?

JOHN: It's okay, you know, it's okay. *(Pause)* So quiet, obviously . . . but I . . . did, I do what you say, and I focus on eh, a small, objective. I stay . . . *(Unsaid: "centered on it")* There were a couple of bills there, or whatever, there on the mat. Okay. Down to the post office, paid that . . . Em . . .

(Pause.)

IAN: And how does it feel in the house? When you're there.

JOHN: In the house, itself? Like I say. I'm aware, I'm wary . . . but in a funny way I . . . I can't . . . I can . . . hardly accept what I saw . . . you know . . . But, I know that I did, and so, obviously . . .

IAN: You're a little . . .

JOHN: I'm a little uneasy.

IAN *(Nods)*: Okay.

JOHN: But that's . . . that's also to do with . . . Like, when Mari was alive, you know, we had . . . stopped communicating. But now . . . she's gone, I really feel like there was a lot of communication. Even though, it wasn't . . . verbal . . . I suppose. I mean, she was there. And I was there. And in that, there's obviously, the presence of . . . you know, a living person, I'm not saying this very well. But I think, you know, I believe that . . . we had a huge importance in each other's lives. You know?

IAN: I don't doubt it for a second.

JOHN *(Very affirmative)*: Yeah. *(Beat)* Yeah. I know.

(Pause.)

You know, when you're young. And you're told about . . .
what to expect I suppose. It is kind of happy ever after. But
it's . . . you know, it's weird to accept what happiness really
is, you know, or what it is . . . nothing is ever like anyone
expects, is it, you know? Like, it's not a fairy tale . . . I mean,
it has to be just kind of ordinary, you know? A bit boring
even, otherwise it's probably not real, you know?

IAN: Yeah . . . ?

JOHN: No, it's, it's just that . . . we probably had it, you know?
I mean when I think of it, really, we . . . we had it all, you
know? But it's, it's hard to . . . accept . . . that this is it. You . . .
you go . . . searching, not *searching*, I wasn't going anywhere
searching for anything, but, I think I was always slightly . . .
waiting . . . you know?

   This is something I probably wouldn't even have admit-
ted before, you know? But maybe I felt that when we were
married, and all settled in and eh . . . maybe even before we
found out that we couldn't, that Mari couldn't, have children, I think that maybe even before that . . . I felt that I had
kind of settled for second best, you know? I mean I mean
I look at it now, and man, these are old feelings. Just fucking
there all the time, for . . . all the way along.

(Silence.)

That's terrible, isn't it?

IAN: You felt what you felt . . .

JOHN *(Slight self-disgust)*: Yeah but, what . . . who the fuck did
I think I was? You know?

(Pause.)

You see, we'd, I think, we'd been slightly left behind, a little bit, you know? All our . . . all our friends, they, you know, they had families. And, that . . . that . . . bound them together, you know? And, you see, I think that that . . . that we were . . . we were slightly left behind a little bit maybe. And that we felt that there was something kind of wrong with us, not anything serious or really wrong, but that there was a whole . . . you know, a whole experience, a whole way, maybe, of . . . of relating to everything, that wasn't . . . it wasn't available to us. (Suddenly) It was a pain in the fucking hole to tell you the truth!

You know. I don't know if you have children, and I don't mean anything, because this is nothing about those people, but you know, I found, we found, that, okay, of course we were invited to places, you know, to parties and everything. But that's what there was to talk about, you know? "Oh my sons are ten and eleven." "Oh my son is eleven!" You know?

And of course! Look, that's what people talk about. Of course they do. It's perfectly normal to want to talk about the things that are happening in your life. But, you know, that was what we were always sort of on the edge of. You know, those conversations. You know, you'd be trying to, waiting for the subject to change and then of course, some stupid fucker would turn around and go, "Do you have any kids, yourself, John?" And I'd be, and I know that this happened to Mari too, I'd be like, "Eh, no, no actually, I don't." Which'd be then . . . "Oh! Right! Okay!" You know?

I mean, I don't know if it felt like a big thing at the time, in a funny way, but it must have been, because I always felt . . . that it . . . wasn't . . . addressed because in a way, maybe I felt that the whole thing should be different—not just that we should adopt some kid or something—but that I should change the whole . . . the whole fucking thing, you know? Start again, somewhere else. Which then, of course, just feels mad and you want to let yourself believe that all these things aren't that important but . . . it was there and . . . what can I say? There was all this shit going on and I . . . our life just carried on and we grew up basically and our childbearing years were over and we got on with it, and that's, but then, out the fucking blue, about three years ago . . .

(Pause.)

I met someone, you know?

(Pause.)

I mean . . . I didn't meet her, we'd already met her, we both had met her, up at a . . . party up there in Howth up there, you know? House of a guy I was doing some business with.
    (Suddenly) This is fucking mad fucking shit, now, you know?
IAN: I know. I know. It's okay . . .
JOHN: Yeah, well, like I say it was someone we'd both seen around a little bit for years. She's wealthy, you know? The husband is loaded, you know? And I suppose just the ordinary feelings of that . . . surface . . . glamour . . . I mean you'd see this woman, there was no doubt about it, she was, you know, the most beautiful woman in the room or whatever, or even wherever you'd go she'd be one of the top five best-looking women there, you know? I mean, that's what we're talking about here, you know? And obviously that's . . . that's very attractive, you know?
    But about three years ago we were invited up to this guy, O'Leary, big hotel guy, up to his mansion up there on Howth Head. And both of us were excited about it and looking forward to it, you know, Mari liked dressing up. She had a good figure and she could, she could definitely hold her own, and this would have been a big deal and we were in good form going up there beforehand. And it was, you know, there were

33

people up there parking the cars for you and all this, you know what I mean? Up these steps like, and butlers standing there with champagne and hot ports and all this, serious stuff now, you know?

And in we go, into this place, serious mansion now, you know? And as usual, you know, we're fucking standing there on our own—fucking, you know, trying to talk to each other, but of course we both wanted to get stuck in and meet some other people and I was dying for a slash and Mari doesn't want to let me go and leave her on her own there, and all that, yeah?

But eventually we get talking to another couple, and a business guy I know comes in and it's warming up and I leg it down to the jacks and kind of—the way it goes, you know, I don't see Mari until everyone sits down later on for something to eat, 'cause when I'm coming out of the toilet and I'm going through the kitchen I meet a few other people who are there, and then I meet this . . . this woman that I'm talking about . . .

Her name is Vivien . . .

And I stop and say hello and, you know, we're standing there at the . . . you know, in the middle of a kitchen, sometimes in those big houses . . .

IAN: An island.

JOHN: Yeah, and there were these stools and it was like we were sitting at a bar somewhere, you know? The champagne keeps coming round, and it's great, you know? Because not only is this woman so beautiful to look at but we're having a brilliant chat, you know? 'Cause I had been in hospital for a few days having this thing done on my sinuses and it was weird because she was asking me about it and no one had asked me anything really, you know, not even Mari, although she had been great and everything and she came to see me every day—but I'd felt just this . . . just this real lonely feeling when I was in there, you know? I don't know

why, or what happened but when I was in there, I just felt a
bit scared and . . . and em . . .

But I'd had these feelings and anyway, for some reason
I mentioned this to . . . to Vivien, and you know, God it just
felt like I was being taken seriously. You know, and the
champagne is coming round and it turns out that Vivien was
in hospital at nearly the same time, you know? And she starts
telling me that . . . she'd had . . . a miscarriage, you know?
And she's telling me all this and she already has four kids
who are teenagers and this pregnancy was out of the blue,
and there'd been all this going on, and it hadn't worked out,
and all this had . . . you know brought up, a lot of things for
her about many things in her life and it's all this and, so like
we're having this big talk, and then, you know, it's an hour
and a half later, and we're all being called in to sit down at
this huge dinner . . . and on the way in, she . . . she takes my
mobile number and puts it in her phone. And although in
one way it just seemed like a normal thing to do, in another
it was . . . you know . . . and I didn't really . . . let on to Mari
that I'd only been talking to Vivien all that time when I got
back, you know, I played up the other people that I'd only
seen or just said hello to.

So we're there and we don't have a great time, because
Mari is pissed off that I'd left her talking to these fuckers she
didn't really know, and of course, about twelve o'clock, she
says she doesn't feel so good, so great! We're the first ones to
leave and we're not talking in the car and it's basically just
one of those, and I'm kind of used to it, you know?

But Christmas, you know, we go over to her folks' house
and do the whole bit, and when I get home, bit tipsy, I'm
upstairs getting changed and I see on my phone, I have a
text. And it's from Vivien and it's, "Great to see you the other
night. Happy Christmas."

So I'm like standing up there in the bedroom, in my
socks, you know, and I'm like some youngfella, and I text her

back, "It was great to see you too," you know, "Happy Christmas."

And some part of me knew, you know? That I was sort of going into something . . . you know? And . . .

(Pause.)

But, you know there were no more texts and . . . but, something had . . . I mean whatever it triggered off . . . you know . . . here I was all of a sudden, just really thinking about this woman. Who . . . in many ways was different to what I knew, you know? And probably the big one was . . . you know . . . that . . . She was a mother.

Whatever that . . . means, you know? But anyway, Christmas was gone, and the new year and all that bollocks, which is a very depressing time of the year as far as I'm concerned and there were no more texts . . . and . . . I don't know what I was expecting to happen but I just got more and more into a filthy mood, over those days. And Mari was asking me what was wrong with me, and I was bulling because I'd erased Vivien's text, and I wanted to look at it again as something to hang on to, which was you know, whatever.

But as usual, Mari dragged me into the Christmas sales because I needed new clothes and we were in fucking . . . Roches Stores or somewhere and . . . I got a text . . . from Vivien, and it was just like, "How are you?" You know? And man, it was like someone had thrown me a rope, you know? I was like, "Thank God!" You know? There's someone in the world who actually cares about how I'm getting on, you know? Like, this was what that meant to me. Crazy fucking shit, you know?

So I slipped off and said I wanted to have a look at some shoes or something, and I texted her back, quickly just saying, "Post-Xmas blues," or something and bang! She texted me right back like, "Hang in there," or something and

that's, it's so fucking stupid, but that's how it continued then
all day really.

IAN: Your wife didn't hear all these texts going off?

JOHN (*Shakes his head*): No, I had the phone on silent, vibrate, in
my pocket, you know? I mean, you know? I was already . . . you
know . . . ?

IAN: Mm. Yeah I know.

JOHN: And of course, suddenly I'm all chipper then, and I take
Mari for her lunch in the Westbury! You know. I'm all
cheered up. That morning she'd seen this bright red coat in
one of the designer shops in Brown Thomas or somewhere.
Reduced from like three grand to two grand or something,
and of course it was still too dear and all that, but after lunch
I took her down and bought it for her, you know? The fucking guilt, you know?

I mean, this is the terrible side of it. That coat was then,
like her good coat from then on, you know?

(*Pause.*)

She was wearing it, you know, the night she was . . . the night
she died, you know?

(*Pause.*)

She had it on when I saw her, you know? Behind the door
there.

(*He exhales deeply.*)

So, but, you know, we went home, life continues. Back to
work, which I was glad about, because, you know, it gave me
more time to myself. You know? Texting Vivien? You know?

IAN: Mmm.

JOHN: And then of course . . .

IAN: What were the texts?

JOHN: Ah, it was just normal stuff, you know? Nothing. "How are you doing?" "Back to work today." "Ah well, keep your chin up!" You know? Nothing—except that it shouldn't have been happening . . . you know, so . . . so then, of course, as time goes on, that's, that's not enough for me . . . ? So . . . I, I text her and say, "Let's have a coffee sometime." And that's opened it up, because, at first I hear nothing, and I think, "Whoa, I've gone too far . . . " But then bang! Like a day later . . . She fucking rings me! Right in the middle of a meeting with these two business guys down in Longford, in the Longford Arms Hotel. And I see her name come up on the phone—so I'm like, "I have to take this." So I go outside and it's like, "God it's great to hear you," you know? It was just . . . it just felt like such a fucking relief, you know?

And she's on for like a big chat on the phone, but I'm like . . . I can't do it, so I kind of cut to the chase, and I say, "Let's meet up!" you know? And she's, you know, suddenly I sense a kind of reluctance, like she's not saying no, but . . . I can just . . . *(Unsaid: "sense it")* But I drive it on and I say, "Let's meet on Friday, get some lunch, just get a quick sandwich somewhere," or something, and she's like, "Where?" And so like, without either of us acknowledging it, I say, "The Killiney Court Hotel," because it's really miles out of the way for both of us, and no one would see us, you know, but of course I don't say that, but I figure she gets it, and I say I'm going to be out that way and so on. All very innocent, like— *(Sarcastic)* "Yeah, right!" But my heart was pounding while I'm talking to her, you know? And I could . . . like the stakes were really going up!

IAN *(Affirmative)*: Well, yeah . . .

JOHN: And . . . I mean, I don't know if you know what it's like, but . . . Having a secret like that from your wife . . . Nothing is as strong as a secret like that, I mean for binding two people. In my *mind* anyway! As far as I was concerned, we were already like two fugitives or something, you know? So, but, we made this arrangement. And of course, the next few days was kind of mad, like, "What am I doing? This is crazy." I was . . . I was just like an actor, or something, in my own life, just playing this part in something that just didn't seem real, you know, or as real as . . . I mean, crazy, you know? Like I felt I could just look behind everything because it was only scenery, everywhere I went. Because, I suppose in a mad way I believed that *something else* was my reality! And that all this other shit—my life!—was . . .

Like I found myself looking at Mari while she was prattling on and thinking, "Who the fuck is this fucking woman?" What's happened? That we live in the same house? There's been some fucking . . . mistake, you know?

IAN *(Affirmative)*: Mmm.

JOHN: So a few days later, Friday, you know, I had cleared the decks, I had nothing else to do so I was over there in Killiney at like twelve o'clock, you know? And it was a horrible day, you know? It never really got bright—didn't rain, but it was . . . almost like GOD KNOWS WHAT YOU'RE DOING . . . you know?

(They both laugh a little.)

And eh . . . we met, you know? *(Suddenly without any defense or guile)* I couldn't believe it when I saw her coming through the door. I just could not fucking believe it, you know? I was like, thank God, you know? Like how can this beautiful woman be coming in here to be with me? You know? This is *real*, you know? God. And she just came in there and she sat down where I was sitting. And she was really nervous too, you know? And she just starts talking, talking, talking. Her kid is in this new school and all this, and her husband is going through this huge deal at work and he's in Japan all the time and she's getting this work done by these builders,

39

and basically all this bollocks that I realize I have no interest in at all! And there was this horrible feeling that all this going on and on was just really a bit annoying, you know? This just wasn't . . . I was selfish basically, and I . . . I wanted this to be more about me, you know?!

(They smile.)

So we got a few hot whiskeys and after I feel like I've been politely listening to all this shite for long enough, I started to move it around more to . . . us being there, and . . . and I knew I was rushing it but . . . I was really just, trying to move it on to the next stage. Because I didn't want the whole . . . illusion of it . . . wrecked. I mean, I was putting everything into this—the whole lot—all the eggs in the one basket, I mean, insane, you know?

And I mean, madly, I just said to her, "Look, I need to . . . be with you, you know? And hold you and . . . " Crazy.

And she just went so quiet then that I thought, okay, I've fucked it, you know, she's . . . you know, she thought this was something else . . . like we were going to be just friends in some . . . bizarre way I don't fucking . . . relate to, you know? And it was three o'clock now and I'd have to start heading soon now anyway, but then she goes, "Yeah, okay, let's . . . " But then I'm like slightly, like, "Don't just do this for me!" You know, like, don't kill yourself . . . But sure, I didn't even know what I was doing, you know?

I was like a robot. But everything I was doing was wrong so nothing made sense, like I got the key, and I was convinced your woman behind the desk was going to call the fucking guards, you know?! And this was before that place closed down, it was between when they had sold it and when they closed it down, there was hardly anyone around. Going up to the room, you know? And we didn't say anything. It was just, it was just . . . frightening really. And we go in and the room was like . . . it was like walking into one of the rooms in *Fawlty Towers* or something, like it was straight out of the 1970s. All brown and pink flowery patterns everywhere. And it was freezing. It was . . . it was horrible.

But. We sat on the bed. And we . . . started . . . sort of . . . kissing, but, I wasn't . . . it was just so obvious that this wasn't what she wanted. And to tell you the truth I was completely out of practice and I . . . tried to put my hand up her skirt and . . . you know, but she just stopped me. And neither of us were . . . it was just a huge mistake. I had fucked the whole thing to hell, really, you know? And I wanted to just go back to before, when we were just going to meet, you know?

But I didn't . . . I wasn't able to . . . quite express that, so . . . I was just sort of apologizing, and really, we both had to go then and . . .

It was just fucking awful to tell you the truth, and there didn't seem to even be time to . . . make it . . . like, to have a drink and work it out or make it okay again. It was just over and we just, said good-bye in the car park, you know? Brilliant.

And of course when I got home, just the distance that I felt between me and Mari, I realized that whatever about the way we might have been before, it was nothing compared to this. This was like the Grand Canyon opening up, you know? I knew that I'd driven an unbelievable wedge . . . between us.

And of course, Mari can tell there's something wrong and she's . . . asking me, is there anything she can . . . She came and started stroking my back saying, "God, those are big heavy sighs, John." You know? So I just said, "Ah it's a thing at work, don't worry about it." Whatever, you know?

But seriously, you know, as the days went on, I mean I wasn't getting any sleep, and I was getting up in the middle of the night and just sitting in the kitchen, and then, not able to go into work.

(Pause.)

It was just so . . . I just felt like a piece of shit, you know?

I mean, I had gone from sharing this—I suppose it was a dream—of a . . . special communication or a secret . . . relationship that . . . and now it was, I mean I just felt like some sort of criminal. And I really felt so isolated and cut off and like there was nothing in my life to look forward to. And I just felt like, I knew then that something bad was going to happen, because I deserved it, because there was like some kind of evil in me, that I did.

IAN: Mari didn't . . . you didn't . . .

JOHN: Well, she just didn't know what to do, because I was just only, barely communicating with her. Because I fucking hate myself by this stage, you know?

And when I think about what I must have done to her. With all the silence and . . .

(Pause.)

I started pretending I had to stay down the country, for work, you know, overnight, but I was really just staying in places just so that I didn't have to deal with the terrible *pressure* of going home, you know? And facing that, and facing myself, and, you know?

I'd just be sitting there in some hotel bar in the midlands, you know? Just smoking cigarettes and looking at football or Man United or whatever—just unable to deal with anything, really. And I just, I had been staying in this place in Kildare and I had to leave and come back to Dublin, because I could only ever justify staying away for a night or possibly two at a push, and I was having a cup of coffee before I hit the road and I picked up this magazine, in a whole rack of old magazines, and I saw an ad for like, an escort service, a brothel. I knew what it was. And . . . I just

needed to . . . connect with something, or someone, you know?
When you're so alone like that . . . and when you feel . . . you
know . . . I just . . . I just dialed the number and this woman
answered and she sounded so nice, and you know, she told
me where to go. To this place on the South Circular Road.
And I fucking drove there, you know? I just . . .

(Long pause.)

IAN: Are you okay?
JOHN: Yeah, it's just, this is terrible.
IAN: No.
JOHN: I just find it so fucking hard . . .
IAN: You're doing so well, John. This is such important work, you
know?

(Pause.)

Do you want to leave it there? We can just sit for a while . . . ?
JOHN: How's the time, are we finished?
IAN: No we have time, but maybe you'd just prefer to . . .
JOHN: Well . . . No, I'll, I'll finish what I . . . I came . . . today
to . . . you know . . .
IAN: Okay.
JOHN: Yeah, so I eh . . . anyway, I went to this place. Which was
something I had never done. And this woman answered the
door, and I was hoping the minute I saw her that she wasn't,
I mean, she was a bit older now . . . And she brought me into
this room. And there was just a couch there, and a shower
over in one corner and some towels on a chair, and she says
that this girl, Jeanette, was going to come in in a minute.
And she says it's thirty euros to be there and then whatever
I work out with Jeanette is between ourselves. And I mean,
I'm already like, God this is, I haven't even met this girl, you
know, but I give this woman thirty euros and she tells me to
relax and take a shower and Jeanette will be in in ten minutes.

So I'm there in this room. And I can hear people in the house, talking or moving around or whatever, and it's a bit, you know . . . but I was hoping that whatever was going to happen was going to give me some relief, you know? Not a sexual thing, I don't . . . *(Unsaid: "think")* Just some . . . I mean, I know it sounds . . . "Oh that's what everybody says . . . " but you know . . .

IAN: No, I know.

JOHN: So I just, fuck it, I took a shower in there . . . in the corner. And I dried myself and . . . then I put my clothes back on!

(They smile briefly.)

And I'm in there maybe fifteen minutes and nothing is happening, you know, so I stick my head out the door, but I don't see anyone, and I decide to wait. And the doorbell goes and I hear the woman bringing in some other guy and she takes him off somewhere. And by this stage . . . I'm like . . . this is just freaking me out, really, but at the same time, like I say, I'm hoping for some . . . you know, I'm hanging in there. So I wait and I hear a bit of movement, and I hear someone leaving so I think maybe it's going to happen now, but then twenty minutes go by so I just, I'm like, forget it.

So I put on my coat and I open the door to go and the woman who let me in is coming down the hall going like, *(Strong Dublin accent)* "What are you doing? Go in and have a shower!" And she comes right up to me and the smell of drink off her, you know? And I'm like, "Look, I'm going to leave it."

And then this guy appears, you know? Like a total skanger. Just with these really dead eyes, you know? And he's like, "What's going on?" And they're much louder than they have to be, if you know what I mean.

And for some reason I . . . just . . . decide. That . . . I'm not gonna take this fucking shit anymore, I've just had enough so although I'm probably definitely on a hiding to nothing, I say, "Give me my thirty euros back . . . " which of course, is madness, you know? But of course this *is* fucking madness, you know?

So she shouts, "We don't owe you any money—we provide the amenities and that's what you were charged for. We don't owe you a fucking penny!" And your man is like, "Come on now, you're either going to have to go in and have a shower or you're going to have to go." But by this stage I suppose these two people represent everything that's wrong with the world to me and it's like I'm . . . I just refuse to accept this, you know? And I'm . . . *demanding* my money back! I just want to have a transaction where some normal rules apply again, you know? And look where I was trying to fucking achieve that! You know?

(They smile.)

And then, I just, before I know it, your man just hits me right in the stomach! And I mean, I'm not fit, and I haven't been in a fight since I was maybe ten or something! But that feeling of being completely winded, of not being able to breathe and being completely paralyzed—it just . . . I just bent over slowly and I could hear this awful groan coming out and it was me making it—you know—completely out of my control. And I just went down and down until I was on my knees on the floor. And I hear your man going, "Now you brought that on yourself." And he was so fucking right, you know?

And then they sat me on the stairs, you know? They were getting a bit worried, because I just could not breathe. She's going like, "What did you hit him for?" And he's saying to me, "You'll be all right, you'll be all right . . . " And I felt fucking grateful! It was so stupid but in a mad way, that's what I wanted! I wanted someone to tell me that things were going to be okay. I mean I was really clinging to the fucking wreckage here now, you know?

(He sighs deeply.)

And . . . I went home. Still completely able to . . . I went in and Mari had my dinner there on the table, you know, chops and peas and potatoes. And the pain in my stomach was . . . I could barely fucking walk, you know? And, of course she . . . the minute she sees me she just . . . she was like, "Oh my God, John, what's happened? Are you all right?"

And I . . . *(He almost starts crying but keeps it together)* I just turned on her, Ian, you know? I just . . . exploded. And I ate the head off her. I was like an animal. And it was just so . . . sudden. She looked so frightened, I had never seen that look, of real fear, and I was doing it! You know?

(He starts crying.)

And, I pushed her up against the wall and I told her, "You're fucking killing me."

And I . . . grabbed her by the shoulders and I shook her. I shook her so hard. I could feel how small and helpless she was. It was a terrible feeling. And I said to her, "Don't fucking speak to me anymore. Don't you dare fucking speak to me." And she just cowered down on the floor—nothing like this had ever happened between us before, you know? And she curled herself up into a little ball there down beside the bin. And the sobs just came out of her, you know? Just the total . . . bewilderment, you know?

(Pause. John is in the deep pit of his self-loathing.)

And after that, like from then on, I couldn't . . . And I just don't understand. How, why I just couldn't have talked to her? She only wanted to help me. But it was like . . . *(Short pause)* I was in a kind of a storm, you know? You're only just barely hanging on, just hanging in there. And I was frightened that she'd, or anyone would . . . see how weak I was. And how . . . disgusting I was. And she'd hate me, you know? Everything just developed into a kind of paralysis. That's the only way I can describe it. You just can't fucking move, you know?

Because, I think I killed her that day, you know? I mean, I didn't kill her. But I might as well have.

I mean, I don't even know where she was going the night that . . . or where she had been. We didn't even speak to each other before she died, she was on her own, you know? I just feel like I just fucking left her alone in the world, you know? If I could have even slept in the bed beside her, maybe that might have even been enough! You know, I . . . I probably didn't even have to say anything . . . And now I can't go back!

(Long pause.)

I just . . . I believe in a way that I probably did it to her, Ian, you know?

IAN: No.

JOHN: And that's probably why I've seen her, you know?

IAN: No. I don't . . .

JOHN: Like she only wanted to fucking help me, you know?

IAN: But it was an accident. She was in an accident.

JOHN: But I . . . I mean I think about it. Where would she have been going? She wouldn't have been out on her own in town if . . . you know . . . And she was so kind, you know? I . . . I mean, is it . . . ? Is it that, in some way, she . . . Is she trying to . . .

IAN: I really don't think that . . .

JOHN: Is she trying to hurt me? Or I mean . . .

IAN: Well you see I'm not convinced that . . .

JOHN: Or maybe I've got it wrong. You know? Maybe I've got the whole thing arseways.

(Pause.)

Maybe she's . . . Maybe she's just trying to save me, you know?

(Lights down.)

Scene Four

A church bell strikes twice in the distance. It is night. The office is in darkness except for what light spills in from the street. We hear someone coming up the stairs. The door opens and Ian comes in and switches on a lamp or two. Laurence comes in and hovers near the door. He is skinny and wears sports gear and sneakers. It is hard to tell if he is thirty and looks much younger or twenty and looks much older. He has a nervous, twitchy energy and seems like he lives from minute to minute. He has a dirty bandage on his right hand.

IAN: Come in. Come in. It's okay. There's no one else. There's no one in the whole building. This is . . . where I work.

(Laurence shuts the door. They stand there. Ian doesn't seem to know what to do.)

Let me eh . . . I think I have eh . . . would you . . . drink a glass of wine?

LAURENCE *(Shrugs)*: . . . Yeah.
IAN: Okay . . . Let me, eh . . . Let me . . .

(He bustles about and finds the bottle Neasa brought. He finds two mugs.)

I say "glass" . . . but . . . I'll just . . . Eh . . .

(He motions to Laurence that he wants to get past him, and he goes into the bathroom to wash the mugs. We hear him in there while Laurence stands alone in the room. He comes back out with the mugs and stops abruptly.)

Corkscrew. Didn't think of that. Didn't think of it. Em.
LAURENCE: You can push it in.
IAN: The . . .
LAURENCE: You can push the cork down. If you have something to . . .
IAN: Like eh . . .
LAURENCE: Just a knife.
IAN: I have a knife. *(He goes to a box which has a few kitchen things)* Just a cutlery knife . . .
LAURENCE: Yeah, just anything . . .

(Ian holds up an ordinary "knife and fork" knife.)

Yeah, you . . .

(He goes to Ian, who takes the bottle up, and they awkwardly jockey for position.)

IAN: Will I . . . or . . . *(He hands the bottle to Laurence)*
LAURENCE: Yeah, you just . . . you push it down. My . . . *(He gestures with his bandaged hand)*
IAN: Oh yes, you just . . . *(He takes the bottle and attempts to push the cork in)*

LAURENCE: If you, just . . . if you take that, tear off the . . .

IAN: Oh yeah, yeah. *(He uses the knife to cut the seal away from around the cork)* Actually I'm going to put it on the . . . Just . . . *(He puts the bottle on the floor and pushes the cork down with the knife)* It's going down.

LAURENCE *(Indicating the bathroom)*: Is that the jacks?

IAN: Oh yeah, go ahead.

(Laurence goes into the bathroom. Ian struggles on the floor. Finally the cork goes in.)

(Calls out) I've done it, it's gone in!

(He pours two mugs of wine. He stands there, waiting. He seems disconnected for a moment, almost not part of his own life. The toilet flushes. Laurence emerges. Ian hands him a drink.)

Now. God, the things we do, ha? Well, cheers

(They drink.)

God, it's all right. Here. *(He gives Laurence another drink)* Is your hand all right?

LAURENCE: Ah yeah. It's wrecked.

IAN: What happened to it?

LAURENCE: Ah, a banger. I was eh . . . I was letting off a banger, with my son, on Halloween. Sometimes my eyes aren't that good. And the fucking thing nearly blew my fucking hand off.

IAN: Oh my God. Is it all right?

LAURENCE: Ah it's wrecked. I can only move these two fingers.

IAN: Oh no.

LAURENCE: Yeah, it's a fucking killer, you know? I can't work, you know?

IAN: Oh no. What, what do you, what, what are you working at
    or . . .
LAURENCE: Ah, I was lined up to get a job driving a van, but . . .
IAN: Oh no.
LAURENCE: Yeah.

(Pause.)

IAN: Is it . . . is it healing or are you getting treatment for it or . . .
LAURENCE: Ah, I'm supposed to keep . . . to go in for physiother-
    apy but, it's, it's tricky 'cause I'm trying to keep a few things
    organized at the moment and I, sometimes . . . the appoint-
    ments don't suit me, then, you know?
IAN: Right . . .
LAURENCE: Because of the times. But this fucking thing is filthy,
    I need to . . . but they keep you waiting for so long in there,
    though, you know?
IAN: God, well . . . God, well you . . . you don't want to let it get
    infected.
LAURENCE: I know. I know. But, yeah, you know, I have to do it.
    You know?

(Pause.)

IAN: Are you cold? Do you want me to turn that, turn that on?
LAURENCE: Yeah, I'm freezing. Are you not cold?
IAN: Oh sure, I'll . . . (He goes and turns on an electric heater) This
    heats up real fast.

(Pause.)

I'd say it gets pretty cold when you're . . . up there just . . .
LAURENCE: Yeah, it's . . . you know . . . but sometimes you just
    fucking have to, 'cause . . .
IAN: Yeah . . . Yeah . . . (Pause) I've never eh . . . I've never gone
    up there, before, you know? I've never . . . this is the . . .

I mean . . . Do you, do . . . I, do you, do I pay you now, or do
I . . . ?

LAURENCE: Yeah, well, whatever. If you want to get it out of the
way, you don't have to think about it then, anymore, you
know?

IAN: Yeah, yeah, that's . . . okay, let's . . . okay. *(He counts out
some money from his pocket)* Em. *(He hands it to Laurence)*
That's . . .

LAURENCE: Yeah. You don't have to be so nervous.

IAN: Yeah. I know. I'm sorry. I just, em . . . I've never . . .

LAURENCE: Because you're making me nervous.

IAN: Oh no, I don't want to, I'm sorry.

LAURENCE: Yeah, no, it's just, I get, like I just . . .

IAN: I know, I know, it's contagious. I know. I've never . . .

LAURENCE *(Indicating sound system)*: Do you want to turn on
some music or something?

IAN: Yeah! Yeah, I'll . . . *(Goes over to the stereo and starts looking
through some CDs)* God, what'll I put on?

LAURENCE: Just whatever you want.

IAN: Yeah, but em . . . Do you like the Eagles?

LAURENCE: Don't know them.

IAN: No. Hold on, someone burned this for me . . *(He puts on a
CD. It is slow, mellow country rock)* This is, you know, it's
quite laid-back.

*(Laurence makes a slight move as though he may be coming
toward Ian. Ian halts him with his voice.)*

You have a son?

LAURENCE: Yeah.

IAN: Is he . . . How old is he?

LAURENCE *(Without much enthusiasm)*: He's six.

IAN: Wow, is he . . .

LAURENCE: He's with his ma. She's nuts, you know, her mother
looks after him more.

IAN: Right.

LAURENCE: Yeah, but look, I don't really wanna . . .

IAN: Yeah, of course, I'm sorry.

(Pause.)

Are you a bit warmer?

LAURENCE: Yeah, yeah.

IAN: God . . . I'd say it's cold up there, though, when you're waiting around, is it?

LAURENCE: Yeah it's weird, you know? I mean, it's a bit . . .

IAN: Mmm.

LAURENCE: Yeah, I got the shit kicked out of me one time up there, you know?

IAN: Oh no . . .

LAURENCE: Yeah, ah it was my own fault. I wouldn't even be out there tonight only, I've been staying with my cousin in this flat in town. But this young one came to stay there, and she said there was some money gone out of her bag, and . . . it wasn't me, like, but . . . now . . . I have to try to . . .

IAN: Yeah . . .

LAURENCE: Get a few quid together.

IAN: I know.

LAURENCE: So I can go back and . . .

IAN: Yeah . . .

LAURENCE: I don't even want to go back, though, but I need an address.

IAN: Yeah.

LAURENCE: This is where you work, yeah?

IAN: Yeah, well, yeah . . . I've been here for a few months, you know?

LAURENCE: What do you work at?

IAN: Well, I'm a therapist, you know?

LAURENCE: A therapist?

IAN: Yeah, you know . . .

LAURENCE: What, do you . . .

IAN: Well, you know, people can come, and . . . talk to me, or . . .

LAURENCE: What, like mad people?

IAN: No, not mad . . . Just maybe . . . people who might just feel a little bit . . . stuck, you know? And maybe they . . . just need a . . . just another point of view on what's going on, if they're carrying, you know, a big burden, you know? Of some guilt maybe. You know? Or where they might feel it's hard to go on because they've got themselves just in a bit of a corner, because they're worried about other people, or maybe it's just that they have some old feeling . . . Maybe even from years ago, just even sometimes things can happen to us when we're children, and that, you know, maybe that sets the tone for how people get on later. Where maybe they get a bit stuck. And maybe I can just invite them to consider something that maybe they didn't think was that important before, but, you know, maybe it was . . . and . . .

LAURENCE: Do you ever hypnotize people?

IAN: No, no I don't. We . . . no, it's, it's all fully conscious. It's . . . about perceiving reality, I suppose.

(Pause. Laurence puts his drink down as if to move toward Ian.)

I have a daughter. That I haven't seen . . . either . . . you know, much . . . She's with her mother . . . I mean, I know what you . . . when you say . . .

(Laurence moves toward Ian. Ian stands very still. Laurence puts his hand on Ian's arm and gently moves him closer.)

LAURENCE: It's all right. Don't be frightened.

(Laurence takes Ian's drink and puts it down. Ian is shaking. Laurence pulls Ian toward him and holds him, swaying to the

music. Ian tentatively puts his arms around Laurence.
Suddenly the music breaks into faster, wholly inappropriate
hillbilly fiddle/banjo music.)

IAN: Sorry!

(He goes to the stereo and turns it off.)

God, that's, look, em . . . when I say that I haven't, you know,
done this, or gone up to the park before, I don't mean that
I haven't just gone up to the park at night, you know . . . I
mean. *(Pause)* I mean I've never been with a man. *(Pause)*
Do you understand me?

LAURENCE *(Shrugs)*: That's all right. The men who go up there
are all fucking married, you know? Loads of them are!
That's why . . . they . . . *(Pause)* What difference does it
make? *(Pause)* You should just do what you want to do, you
know? *(Pause)* Put on the other music. Put on the music that
was on before. *(Reassuringly)* I have nowhere else to go.

(Ian puts on the other music. He goes to the bottle and pours
them both another drink. He hands a mug to Laurence, avoid-
ing eye contact. Laurence takes his hand. Ian looks into
Laurence's eyes. Laurence returns his gaze. They move closer
together.
Lights down.)

SCENE FIVE

It is daytime. Bright sunlight streams into the room. As the scene progresses, the room should become more dusky. There are dust sheets on the desk and most of the furniture and books are gone. There are boxes all around the office. Ian is on the floor, gift-wrapping a child's teddy bear with great difficulty. There is a little transistor radio on the floor and indistinct daytime radio is playing while Ian packs. The intercom buzzer goes off and Ian goes to answer it, maybe a bit pissed off; he doesn't expect anyone.

IAN: Yeah? Hello? Hello? Yeah, hold on. *(He presses the buzzer to release the door)* Hello? Are you in? Hello? What? Hello? *(He presses the button again)* Hello? Are you there? What?

(There is a knock on his door. Ian opens it to reveal John, carrying a present.)

Oh, hello!

JOHN: Sorry, I'm barging in on you.

IAN: No! No! I just I couldn't hear . . . come in, come in!

JOHN *(Coming in)*: No, I just . . . I've had this, fucking . . . I've had it in the car and I, 'cause I wanted to get you something.

IAN: Oh no!

JOHN: And then, of course, I've been driving around with it in the boot for the last six weeks, you know what I mean?

IAN: Oh no . . .

JOHN: It's nothing.

IAN: Oh no . . .

JOHN: It's a lamp, it's nothing.

IAN: Oh but still, thanks, you . . . come in, sit down, there's nowhere to sit.

JOHN: And I was going by, and I thought . . . God, I should just call in, and I thought, well, it's lunchtime, he probably won't have anyone there, and . . .

IAN: No, no, I'm . . .

JOHN: Janey Mack, you're . . .

IAN: Well, no, it's lucky you . . . I'm moving! I'm going, you know?

JOHN: You're moving your office?

IAN: I'm, well, no, I'm moving. I'm, I'm going down to Limerick, believe it or not.

JOHN: Limerick?

IAN: Yeah, my fiancée is there and . . . *(As though these are tedious little details that are too boring to go into)* With our . . . baby, and some . . . friends of hers have lent her a house there, so . . .

JOHN: Yeah.

IAN: I'm going down . . . and I've, you know, I'm applying for a . . . I've an interview down there. For a post so . . .

JOHN: Yeah.

IAN: Mmm. You know, so . . . it's time, and . . .

JOHN: Yeah, well great! That sounds good. Dublin's . . . you know . . .

IAN: Yeah.

JOHN: It's a tough town.

(Pause.)

IAN: Yeah, well, look, let me, move some of this stuff. Sit down! *(He bustles around)*
JOHN: Ah, I'm not gonna stay, really.
IAN: No, no! Look, the kettle is still . . . on the go, we're still . . . Let me . . . *(Disappears into the bathroom with the kettle. Off)* So, how are you keeping?
JOHN: Yeah. You know, I'm good! You know, I have to say, I'm good. Thank God, you know? I'm getting there, you know, definitely, and I really, you know . . .

(Ian reemerges and plugs the kettle in.)

I just wanted to say thanks, because, you know . . .
IAN: No, no. You did the work, you know?
JOHN: Yeah, no, but, you know, I mean . . . I wanted to, you know . . .
IAN: God, well, you didn't have to. And you shouldn't have. Really, you know?
JOHN: Yeah, well . . .
IAN: No, well, thank you, I mean . . . will I open it?
JOHN: Yeah, yeah! Go ahead, open it, it's nothing, you know? It's really, it's not . . .

(Ian starts to open the gift.)

I mean, I have no eye for these things. The girl in the shop, you know, I—it was her really. I mean, I said it was a present and she said, who is it for, and then of course I realized, "God, I know nothing about this man!" You know? *(They laugh)* Because I don't! I mean, it's weird, isn't it?
IAN: Well, it's, you know, it's . . . *(Unsaid: "normal")*

JOHN: So I said, it was just a thank-you present really.

IAN: Tch, God, no . . .

JOHN: And she . . .

(Ian produces a stunning antique lamp from the box.)

IAN: Oh my God!

JOHN: Ah, no, sure . . .

IAN: This is too much.

JOHN: No, it's nothing.

IAN: Is it, it's . . . an antique, or . . . ?

JOHN: It's, ah, it's from the thirties or fucking something, I don't know.

IAN: No, well that's, it's too much . . .

JOHN: Please, no. Do you like it?

IAN: It's beautiful, really . . .

JOHN: Well, you know, thank you, you know, that's . . . *(Unsaid: "why I'm here")* I . . .

IAN: Thank you, really, thanks, God . . .

JOHN *(Producing a card from his pocket)*: And this is just a little card. You know, to go . . .

IAN: Oh, God . . . God, thanks, thanks John, really. *(Reads the card)*

JOHN *(Interrupting Ian reading it)*: Ah, read it later.

IAN: Tch. God, no, well. I don't know what to say now.

JOHN: Ah there's . . . *(Unsaid: "nothing to say")*

IAN: God, well let me make you a cup of tea. Here, sit down, take off your coat.

JOHN: I'm grand, really.

IAN *(Producing an old stool from somewhere)*: No, sit down there, here.

(John sits a bit awkwardly.)

So, God, how are you keeping?

JOHN: I'm good, you know? I'm good. I'm . . . I've just bought an apartment.

IAN: Oh wow, so we're both . . .

JOHN: We're both moving. Yeah . . . nearly finished the, the legal . . . which can be a nightmare . . . but it's . . . it's . . .

IAN: If it's what you've got to do, that's right, I know . . .

JOHN: Yeah, it's lovely. It's down there on the seafront, just there near St. Anne's Park.

IAN: Oh very nice, yeah, I know there.

JOHN: Yeah, it's those ones there . . .

IAN: They're nice, yeah.

JOHN: Yeah, so whole new . . .

(Ian finds teabags and cups.)

IAN: And you're . . . You're good . . . in yourself, and . . .

JOHN: I'm . . . really good, Ian, you know? I have to say. I'm looking forward to the move. And I've . . . actually been in the house again, this last month, you know?

IAN: Oh right! God, that's . . . do you take sugar?

JOHN: No, no, it's fine.

IAN: Good, because I don't . . . eh . . .

(They laugh a little.)

JOHN: No I don't, anyway, so . . . and eh, yeah, I've been there, in the house. And I mean, there was a time, as you know, I couldn't even have envisaged myself spending even one night there, so, no I'm . . .

IAN: But you're going to move on and . . .

JOHN: I'm moving on . . . It's, it's just . . . It just feels right. It just feels like that's, that's what . . . I . . . what I . . . that's just what I want to do! I mean, I don't want to be some old guy on his own in there. You know? That house is all to do with me and Mari, and it's even too big for two people—it was too big when we moved in. I mean, if there had been kids, okay, but, you know, that didn't happen and . . . I mean, I just feel like my life isn't over, you know? Like why should I stay in the house out of some kind of mad fucking duty to fucking . . . you know . . . I mean . . .

IAN: I know, you're right, I know. I mean it's so . . .

JOHN: I mean we create these fucking . . .

IAN: I know, I know . . .

JOHN: These mad . . .

IAN: I know. I know. But that's, you know, that's great, you're . . .

JOHN: Yeah . . . I'm . . . you know, I'm getting on with it, and I really see it now like a . . . like a new chapter is opening up, and like *you* know, there was a time I could never have thought that that was even possible! You know, I mean . . .

IAN: Well, that's great, I mean, that's . . .

JOHN: And that's why, I mean, I want to thank you really, because . . .

IAN: Yeah, well, like I say, you did the work.

JOHN: . . . I don't know what I . . . would've . . .

IAN: Well, look I'm . . . I'm glad. I'm happy for you, I mean that. And, you know, I hope, you know, you . . .

JOHN: My fucking brother introduced me to a woman, there, you know?

IAN: Oh . . . ?

JOHN: Yeah, I mean, he's a prick. He can be a bit of an arsehole. But he's, you know . . . he's all right, you know, really.

IAN: Yeah, I know what you mean.

JOHN: Yeah, him and his missus were killed asking me over for some dinner there four or five weeks ago. I was like . . . *(Sarcastic)* "Yeah, right . . . " you know. Because I can sometimes do without that, you know what I mean? But I . . . went over. There were a few people there. This girl was there. I knew her, though, slightly, from before, she used to work where I—she used to work there, coincidentally, and she's . . . she's a bit younger than me now, you know, but . . .

IAN *(Shrugs)*: Well . . .

JOHN: Yeah, sure, what fucking difference does it make? I agree. Although . . . if she was a good bit *older* than me now, the shoe might well be very much on the other fucking foot now, you know what I mean?

(They laugh.)

No, but, she's a nice girl, you know? Sure, I'm not . . . we just went to the pictures and had a drink, you know, just . . . *(Short pause)* We're going to the theatre tomorrow night.

IAN: Oh!

JOHN: I know! *(As though the theatre is rubbish)* "Good luck!" Ah, but, sure . . .

IAN: Yeah, well, that's . . . *(Short pause)* Don't feel that you have to rush into anything, John, you know?

JOHN: No, no, no, no, I'm not, no. I'm, it just feels like it's just a part of . . . just a new . . . it's all just a new . . . it's good, you know? Don't worry.

IAN: Yeah, yeah, no, I'm . . .

JOHN: But Jesus! Do you know who I saw?

IAN: Yeah?

JOHN: Vivien.

IAN: Yeah?

JOHN: Vivien, the . . .

IAN: Yeah.

JOHN: The object of my . . . my downfall. The big . . .

IAN: Yeah.

JOHN: Yeah, saw her there at a do. God, it was weird, you know? I mean she had great sympathy for me and everything, but it was really like nothing had ever happened? Between us? Weird, you know? And do you know what was really weird? I realized we had *nothing* in common. What about that, you know?

(Ian nods.)

63

Serious. Serious fucking shit. I came away thinking, "I don't even like this woman," you know? Bizarre. When I . . . *(Short pause)* Mad.

(Pause.)

IAN: God, John. Well, you know, it sounds like you're doing really well though, you know?
JOHN: Well, I'm, you know . . .
IAN: But you're getting out, you're meeting people . . . and . . .
JOHN: Ah, I'm just, I'm just taking it handy. And . . . it was a great help, you were a great help, Ian, to me, you know? I mean it and . . . I wish you all the best, you know?
IAN: Well, look, I wish you all the best too, John. I really do, you know, and . . . you know, it makes me feel good to see you . . . that you're, you know . . .
JOHN: Well, thanks. Thank you. You know? *(Short pause)* And I'll . . . I only came to . . . I better let you . . . .
IAN: Well, I'm, yeah . . . I said I'd drop the keys back this afternoon and . . . I'm . . .
JOHN: Do you want a hand with anything?
IAN: No, no, no . . .
JOHN: Are you sure?
IAN: Really, don't . . . I'm, I'm nearly there now.

(They are standing. John picks up his coat.)

JOHN: Okay.
IAN: So, no ghosts.
JOHN: No. No ghosts. *(He exhales)* But, I'll tell you, you know, even if I saw one, Ian, it's not . . . I mean, seeing something is one thing but . . . it's how it makes you *feel*, isn't it? It's how that makes you feel. That's what's important. Someone could see something and it doesn't really matter. Someone else'll see it and . . . it's the end of the world, you know?

IAN *(Affirmative)*: Mmm.

JOHN: That's the reality, you know? What it *does* to you is the reality.

IAN: I know.

JOHN: But you don't believe in ghosts anyway, Ian. You've got it sussed.

(They are moving toward the door.)

IAN: John, there was a time I would've given anything to see one. Just to know that there was . . . something else. Do you know what I mean?

JOHN: Sure.

IAN: Just something else, besides all the . . . you know . . . the pain and the confusion. Just something that gave everything . . . *some* meaning, you know? I'm talking about God, really, you know?

JOHN: I know. Where is He?

IAN: I know. But don't get me wrong. I think you had a real experience. I think you really experienced something—but I think it happened because you needed to experience it.

JOHN: Yeah, I know . . .

IAN: You were pulling all this . . . you felt maybe you couldn't move on without being . . . punished somehow and . . .

JOHN: I know.

IAN: It happened! But . . . I don't believe you saw a ghost. Does that make sense?

JOHN: Well, yeah, it makes sense to me now, but there was a time it really wouldn't have, you know? *(Pause)* But that was a different time.

IAN: Yeah, it was.

JOHN *(Opening the door)*: I'll tell you, the mind, it's mad isn't it?

IAN: John, we know nothing. We just know nothing really.

JOHN: We're just barely fucking hanging in there, really, aren't we?

IAN: Well, some better than others. But you're doing good, John, you know? Considering, I mean, you know?

JOHN: I know. I know that. But I had to fucking go there to find that out. Do you know what I mean?

IAN: I do. I know.

(Pause.)

JOHN: Look, I'll love you and leave you. Good luck with everything, all right?

IAN: Well you too, and thanks, for the present. It really is so thoughtful—

JOHN *(Interrupting)*: Ah, it's nothing, good luck.

(They shake hands.)

I'll see you.

IAN: Well . . . Actually, I'll wait here till you get out down there. And I can buzz it if . . . 'cause it's still . . .

JOHN: Oh, nothing changes! I'll see you Ian, good luck.

IAN: I'll see you, John, bye now.

(Ian hovers near the open door while John goes down. He picks up a flyer off the floor at the threshold and crumples it up. He picks up two books off the floor and looks at the back of one of them. We hear the outer door slam shut. In the distance we hear the faint sound of an ice-cream van's music.)

(Calls out) Did you get out?

(There is no answer.

Ian throws one of the two books in a box near the door. He shuts the door and crosses the room to throw the other book in a different box.

In the darkening gloom of the afternoon, we see that Mari's ghost has appeared behind the door. She is looking at Ian, just as John described her; she wears her red coat, which is filthy, her hair is wet. She looks beaten up. She looks terrifying.

Ian has his back to her at his desk, going through some old mail. But he seems to sense something and turns.

Lights down.)

END OF PLAY

Come On Over

Production History

Come On Over was first performed at the Gate Theatre, Dublin, on September 27, 2001. The director was Conor McPherson; the designer was Eileen Diss and the lighting design was by Mick Hughes. The cast was as follows:

MATTHEW	Jim Norton
MARGARET	Dearbhla Molloy

CHARACTERS

MATTHEW, fifties
MARGARET, fifties

There are two chairs onstage.

    Matthew and Margaret enter together from the same side.

    They both wear plain clothes and hoods. The hoods should look like mass-produced sacking and have neat holes for the eyes and mouth.

    Margaret might wear a simple silver-chain necklace.

    They sit and regard the audience.

MATTHEW

There were tomato plants spiraling up these sticks there in the window ledge.

The sunlight was coming in through all the leaves.

Me and Margaret were looking at them and counting the tomatoes.

I was shocked at how she'd aged.

We'd hardly said a thing since I came in. In off the main street and into her narrow hallway and up the stairs into the spare room.

Her daughter had planted these tomatoes before she'd left to go on her travels.

Margaret watered them and I put my suitcase down and sat on the bed.

Outside, the little town was dead.

So many shopfronts boarded up.

The silence was overwhelming.

The house where I grew up was gone.

I'd stepped off the bus into my past.

Into the shocking reality of myself and everything I'd been through.

Margaret turned away from the plants towards me and took my hand for a moment before she left and I heard her go downstairs.

I'd spent the last two months recovering from an experience I'd had in Africa.

I'd slept and dreamed and prayed in a seminary in Belgium until Father Sebarus came to see me.

He was as sympathetic as always but also businesslike because he was my boss.

He held an A4 envelope on his lap while he sat there gravely talking to me.

I didn't feel any terror anymore, but even though I was medicated I sensed that the envelope would change me even further than I'd already gone.

Maybe even back to what I had been.

MARGARET

I was watering Nuala's tomatoes.

Matthew. Father Matthew sat behind me on the bed.

I stood looking down at them much longer than I needed to because I was starting to cry.

He seemed so old.

This boy I once knew.

And the tomatoes were reminding me, do you see, of a day thirty-odd years ago when we'd taken a walk in the rose gardens in the park. It was October and it was the last of the roses.

He was always huddled in his big coat and I'd always have my hand in his pocket. Holding his hand.

And I loved him so much.

I always remember that day, in the rose gardens.

With the roses dying. And him miles away.

And me wanting to tell him that I'd worn a skirt instead of trousers because I wanted him to touch me.

But I knew I'd already lost him.

He was lost.

MATTHEW

Father Sebarus wanted me to look into this one for a few reasons. Well namely the main one was because it had happened in the town I was born in.

He opened the envelope and in it were photographs of a little girl, maybe thirteen or fourteen.

She was asleep and someone had placed blue flowers all around her. She was a corpse.

She'd been found in the graveyard at St. Monica's, the parish I'd grown up in.

They'd sold some land there and when they were moving some coffins, hers had burst open.

And everyone nearly died.

Because she was perfectly preserved.

She'd been buried four hundred years ago.

MARGARET

Matthew was a Jesuit. He was a scientist.

He'd been all over the world looking into what I suppose people thought were miracles.

He was a very rational sort of person.

And although I hadn't seen him for many years I could tell from his letters that he was reluctant to give his imprimatur that he had ever come across anything that was really a miracle. I suppose he saw a rational cause for everything.

And he'd always been like that.

I was shocked naturally when he said he thought he had a vocation all those years ago.

But there had always been a kindness in him. And I loved him for it.

And he was so courageous taking such a huge step.

I respected him, naturally, and I supported him.

But I don't think I need to tell you that it broke my heart.

MATTHEW

I had a restless night.

It was deathly quiet.

But more than that it was a quiet I'd grown up with, and at about three or half-three in the morning I went into the bathroom and took some toilet roll.

And I took it back into my room and I cried my fucking eyes out, till I thought I couldn't breathe.

I thought then that I heard Margaret stirring so I put the light out and I waited until it started to get bright and I began to feel slightly better.

Almost dreading and wanting to get to work.

A car was picking me up at eight.

And it's not good for a man to lie there all night terrified.

It's not right.

MARGARET

I had his breakfast ready at seven.

He came down all neat and shaven.

But he couldn't really eat.

When I'd ran the B and B, anyone that passed through, the salesmen'd usually go to town on the brekkie, so I was, it was a bit of a habit. I was piling toast and eggs and the best of rashers and sausages in front of him. But he just drank some tea.

Apologizing to me. Always apologizing. But all he did was smoke Silk Cut reds and drink his tea.

His leg was shaking under the table.

So I ignored him and left him to his smoke and his tea, and I sat in the drawing room with that old clock ticking till I heard his car arrive and the mad scratch of his chair on the kitchen floor like God Himself had come to save him.

MATTHEW

They'd left the body in the little church.
You could see all our breaths.

The chap from UCD's phone kept going off. He was saying something about organic substances buried below the permafrost. A woman from Trinity supervised students taking soil samples. But I felt detached.

Because something else was happening.

This child. She just looked asleep.

Her fair hair and the flowers around her.

The only clue was her sunken eyes.

And my hands shook outside while Father Sebarus gave me a light. And it wasn't just the shock of something so weird and out of the ordinary.

It was . . . I knew I'd just laid eyes on the most beautiful thing I'd ever seen.

And so much of me was longing not to be inspired because . . . well, because I'd lost my faith a long time ago. And something in me was begging to be free.

And Father Sebarus was looking at me so intently that I had to turn away and walk through the gravestones because if I didn't I was going to turn and smash his face in.

MARGARET

My husband, Patrick, died from leukemia in hospital in Galway. I was with him when he died.

He was hardly there anymore.

He was a good man. Big fingers like potatoes. A big man. But in the end he was just skin and bone.

I sort of wanted to get into the bed there with him at the end. Sort of to remind myself what it was like to share a bed with someone. Under the covers. A man and a woman. What brings them together, you know? I wanted to see what it was like again. I wanted everyone to go. I was holding his hand when he went.

Nuala finished in UCG and went off on her travels.

I looked after Patrick's father. We looked after each other. He wasn't a bother.

Always asking me why I'd get so fret up about things.

"Sit down there now and have a cup of tea," he'd say.

He'd peel an orange the way he used to when Nuala was a toddler, giving her bits while she pootered around, coming over, getting orange all over his lap.

He'd lean on his stick and look out the window in the kitchen.

He'd trace his finger 'round the edge of the ashtray.

And I'd write to Father Matthew, knowing how much he needed kind words, out there somewhere in South America or some-where, knowing how much he needed, well, the same as what I felt Nuala needed when she rang from Boston or San Francisco. And how much she missed her dad.

And her granddad.

And it was always around these times that I took down all the net curtains to wash them. I don't know why. Like a stupid candle in the bloody window.

MATTHEW

I went back on my own that night.

A little sacristan called Jerry opened the chapel for me. I can't forget the stars.

They were above us and down all across the graveyard.

He turned on the lights and left me there to pray.

But it wasn't really prayer.

I was just thinking about the corpse.

I . . . loved her.

It was like she'd traveled this long distance. All this way, so I could see her.

You see, I was so alone. And I needed to see her again.

But they'd packed her in a thermal case and taken her to Dublin.

I'm a racist.

Blacks and whites age differently.

To me they do.

MARGARET

I have no problem saying this.

I had one of Matthew's V-neck sweaters up to my face.

When I sucked in I was breathing him in through my nose.

The tops of my legs were leaning against his bed.

I folded it for him and lay it with his few clothes.

Taking in his washing I'd looked up and never seen so many stars.

I went into the kitchen, turned off the light in the yard, and came back out in the dark.

I'd got into this habit. Of doing whatever I felt like.

Ha-ha. There was a dance the Pioneers had in Jamestown every month.

I always went and danced with my seventy-year-old bachelor who wasn't a Pioneer at all.

They actually always had drink there for him!

I put my nose on his shoulder and took in all the turf and cigarettes.

Slow waltz. Lovely.

Whatever I felt like.

But. Em. Smelling jumpers in my own house.

MATTHEW *(To Margaret)*: I was lost.

MARGARET *(To Matthew)*: Stop. —Keep going, I'm sorry.

MATTHEW *(To audience)*: Something dreadful happened to me.

MARGARET *(To Matthew)*: Matthew . . .

MATTHEW *(To Margaret)*: You don't understand.

MARGARET *(To Matthew)*: I . . . didn't mean to interrupt you. I'm sorry. I didn't think I was going to.

MATTHEW

(To audience) When I was in Africa, I . . .

I went to the home of an Englishman to . . . to talk with him. Because he'd been . . . seeing a girl. A young girl. A child.

I suspected that he was . . . abusing her.

She was eleven. Her name was Patience.

I'd first seen her under a tree in the shade where she was helping a nurse inoculating babies and children from the school.

She was a bright girl.

She seemed older.

She looked like a woman. I mean a small grown woman.

It was the nurse who told me. Her suspicion about Patience and this English gentleman.

And you see, my faith was very strong then.

I mean I knew why we were here.

We were here to love God.

God was the law. God was the word.

(To Margaret) We don't even have time for this!

MARGARET

(To Matthew) Well. Go on. Because I have things to say.

MATTHEW

(He regards Margaret, then regards the audience. He reaches into his pocket and takes out a box of tablets. He drops them. He picks them up and drops them again a few times during the following:)

When I drop these tablets. They fall to the ground.

I know that when I let them go, they'll never float up into the air or stay hanging where I release them.

They'll always fall to the ground.

Always. And I know why.

I'd spent thirty years, more, just reflecting.

And the idea I had, the idea I had which became the truth for me, was that the tablets or anything I let go of will fall to the ground because something wants them to.

Something is willing the way things are.

The way everything is.

And that will is God.

This was quite plain to me. It was just that simple.

I don't claim that I've always been in my right mind but years
and years in the library . . .

Years and years of order . . .

I don't want to say that it was just seductive.

Because I wasn't weak.

But I had drawn my own conclusions. And I believed in what
I believed in. I had beliefs.

And I went to the home of this Englishman and I confronted
him.

And I was almost manic in my fervor because I knew what I was
talking about.

He went pale, staring at his carpet and his pool.

But ultimately I pitied him and I shook his hand and I left.

But going down the dirt road, I began to see waves in front of my
eyes.

It was the beginning of a migraine.

I could only see anything on the right-hand side of my vision.

And I saw Patience on the road coming towards me, going up to the Englishman's house.

I wanted to stop her and talk to her. We spoke often and we were very close.

But my headache was becoming crippling and I just smiled and walked past her. And she stopped and watched me march by.

All I cared about was getting into a dark room and putting a cold cloth on my head.

So I went to bed and my housekeeper brought me some tea and I slept.

But something woke me.

It was dark. It was dusk. Someone was in the room.

I was groggy and I turned on the lamp.

Patience had let herself in. She had a key.

I . . . pulled back the covers, telling myself again for the tenth time that this'd be the last time.

I was waiting for her to get in.

And she shoved a big knife into my face.

She shoved it in and out four times.

I lost this eye and half my nose and the knife ended up embedded in between my teeth, in my gum here.

She couldn't get it out again, which is what saved me.

MARGARET

He was due to go up to Dublin in the morning.

And we sat eating our dinner.

Pork chops.

And I just came out with it.

I asked him to stay.

I said stay here.

Do you remember, I said, do you remember it was one St. Brigid's Day and all the Holy Faith girls had the day off. I had a skirt on. We went for a walk in the rose gardens. It was October, all the roses were dying.

You broke my heart.

MATTHEW

That can't be right, I said.

St. Brigid's Day isn't in October. It's in the spring.

MARGARET

Whatever. I heard him toss and turn until about one or half-one. He went to the toilet five or six times.

I was dropping off when I felt his weight on the bed.

He was sitting there and I put my hand out and I rubbed his shoulders for a while.

And he lay down with his back to me and I kept rubbing him till he calmed down and his breathing became a bit slower. Then I put my arm around his tummy.

(She takes off her hood.)

And I could feel his . . . He was hard. He was gently pressing it against the inside of my arm here.

MATTHEW *(To Margaret)*: Put it back on.

MARGARET: And I felt the knot where he'd tied the top of his pajama bottoms. I was picking at it.

MATTHEW: I'm not denying any of this but I think you should put it back on.

MARGARET: I gripped him as hard as I could. It was my left hand and I'm right-handed. And while he . . . pushed himself back and forth these were the thoughts I had:

MATTHEW: Please put it back on.

MARGARET: His was the first erect penis I'd touched when I was a girl. And Patrick's was the next and here I was holding it again and I was wondering where it had been.

MATTHEW: Margaret . . .

MARGARET: And I was thinking about Nuala and how many she'd felt.

MATTHEW: Margaret . . .

MARGARET: She's in New York. I don't care what you say about how cheap it is to fly anywhere. She's thousands of miles away and I want to see her. I want her here.

MATTHEW: Margaret, put your hood on.

MARGARET *(To Matthew)*: You're no good. —I'd take you in. I don't care about your face.

MATTHEW: Don't do this to yourself.

MARGARET: You coward.

(She regards him. She finally puts the hood back on.)

MATTHEW

In the morning, before I left, there was a call.

The body had started to rot.

It was decomposing in Dublin.

(Pause.)

When Patience attacked me I was a sinner.

MARGARET: You coward.

MATTHEW: But the greatest sin was to feel abandoned. And not to trust in God's love.

MARGARET: You coward.

MATTHEW: Not to trust in God.

MARGARET: Love me.

MATTHEW

Not trusting God was my greatest sin.

But He sent me this little girl.

Preserved for hundreds of years. To forgive me.

MARGARET

No . . .

MATTHEW

It was His way of forgiving me.

And I knew I had to hurry.

Because I was going to say I'd finally seen a miracle.

And I knew I'd probably have a fight on my hands.

So I got moving.

(*Margaret gets up and goes to Matthew.*
She embraces him.
He leans his head into her.)

END

Conor McPherson was born in Dublin in 1971 and attended University College Dublin, where he began to write and direct. He co-founded the Fly by Night Theatre Company, which performed new plays in Dublin's fringe venues.

Published plays include *Port Authority*: *Rum and Vodka*; *St. Nicholas*; *The Good Thief*, which won a Stewart Parker Award; *This Lime Tree Bower*, which won a Thames TV Award, a Guinness/National Theatre Ingenuity Award and the Meyer-Whitworth Award; *The Weir*, which won the Most Promising Playwright Award from both the *Evening Standard* and the Critics' Circle, and the Laurence Olivier Award for Best Play, ran for eighteen months in the West End of London and played successfully on Broadway; and *Dublin Carol*, which was nominated for both Best Production at the 2000 Dublin Theatre Festival and the 2000 *Irish Times*/ESB Best Play award.

His script for *I Went Down* won Best Screenplay at the San Sebastian Film Festival. *Saltwater*, which he wrote and directed, won numerous European awards, including the CICAE Award for Best Film at the Berlin Film Festival. Mr. McPherson lives in Dublin.